This book belongs to

_____

This book is dedicated to my children - Mikey, Kobe, and Jojo.

Ninja Life Hacks™

Patient Ninja

By Mary Nhin

Pictures by
Jelena Stupar

Patient Ninja had great control over his impulses. He could delay his happiness for a bigger reward later.

For example...

If he had a choice between playing video games or studying for his test, he chose to study so he could be prepared.

When Patient Ninja wanted to buy a new game, he would remind himself that he had a goal to get a new bike.

While working on a craft project, he worked carefully and slowly so the final product would come out right.

But patience didn't come naturally to him. It was something he learned and practiced over time.

Once upon a time, Patient Ninja couldn't wait for anything, and oftentimes he would rush.

When Patient Ninja had a math test, he hurriedly worked through the problems because he loved math.

This caused him to make costly mistakes. When he received his graded work back, he was sad that he got most of them wrong.

During class, Mrs. Brown asked everyone to take turns sharing their recent weekend activity, but Patient Ninja got too excited.

Instead of waiting his turn, he interrupted Confident Ninja. This made the teacher and his friend upset.

While playing a board game, even though it was Calm Ninja's turn to roll the dice, Patient Ninja grabbed the dice and knocked over the entire game.

Patient Ninja felt bad, but he was so excited and couldn't wait.

Would you like to know too? Okay, lean in real close...

Think of patience as a muscle you can strengthen with practice. To make our patience muscle strong, we can build it by practicing the three Ts:

We can *think* through the consequences by asking ourselves questions.

We can practice patience by *taking* some deep breaths.

If we can wait, we'll be rewarded at the end so it helps to *tell* ourselves...

That afternoon, Mrs. Brown said they were making ninja
fidget spinners and they had to work in pairs.

The two worked really hard to make the best fidget spinners possible.

After picking out his ninja fidget spinner shape, Patient Ninja traced his shape carefully onto his paper.

Think through the consequences.

Take *some deep breaths.*

He took a few deep breaths before slowly cutting out his shapes.

Then, he glued his pieces together and waited
patiently for the glue to dry.

Tell yourself, "Good things come to those who wait".

After the finishing touches, the ninjas spun their ninja fidget spinners.

All the spinners worked well but Patient Ninja's and Calm Ninja's spinners spun the best.

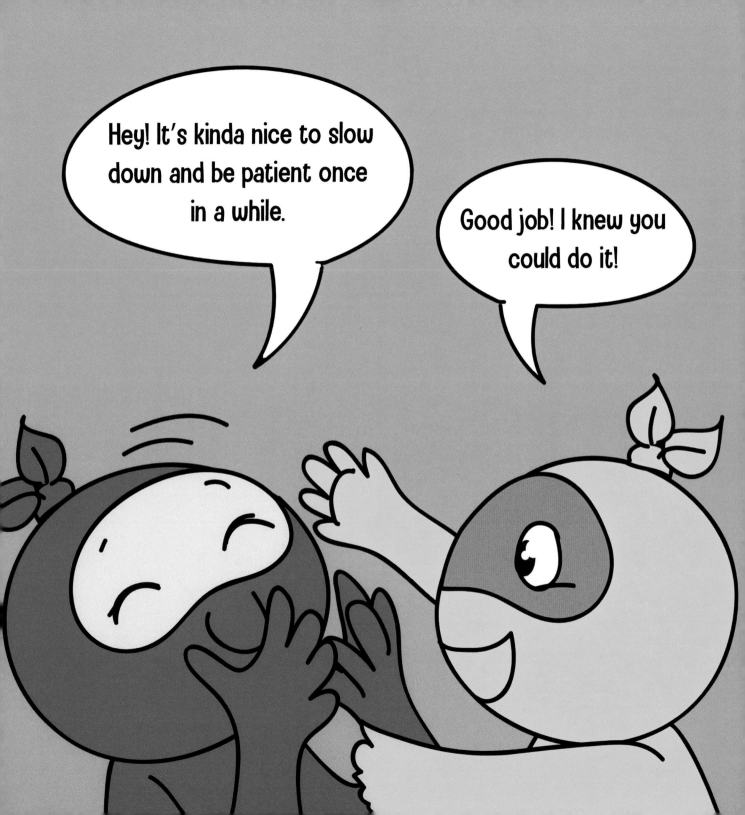

Remembering the three Ts could be your secret weapon against impatience.

Download the Ninja Fidget Spinner template
at **NinjaLifeHacks.tv**

or check out the Ninja Life Hacks Journal
on Amazon to grow your patience today.

@marynhin @GrowGrit
#NinjaLifeHacks

Mary Nhin Grow Grit

Grow Grit

Made in the USA
Coppell, TX
21 December 2020